The Worm Farmer's Handbook: From Beginner Composting to Building a Profitable Worm Farming Business

Anita J. Maddox

All rights reserved. Copying any part of this publication without permission from the author is strictly prohibited except for citations for critical use.

Copyright Anita J. Maddox

Table Of Content

Introduction: Worm Farming, Sustainability, and You

Chapter 1: The Basics of Vermiculture

Chapter 2: Setting Up Your Worm Bin

Chapter 3: Harvesting Worm Castings

Chapter 4: Advanced Worm Farming Techniques

Chapter 5: Turning Worm Farming into a Side Business

Chapter 6: The Role of Worm Farming in Sustainable Gardening

Conclusion: Recap of the benefits, motivation for staying committed, and a final push toward sustainability.

Introduction

The Soil Health Revolution: Worm Farming, Sustainability, and You

What if I told you that the food scraps you toss out every day could become the most valuable thing in your garden? Well, that's exactly what happens when you let a bunch of worms do the heavy lifting.

Worm farming (or **vermiculture**, if you're feeling fancy) is one of the easiest and most effective ways to turn kitchen waste into rich, nutritious compost. It's like having your very own underground crew that takes your leftovers and magically transforms them into what gardeners call "black gold"—but trust me, there's no magic here, just nature doing what it does best.

Welcome to **The Worm Farmer's Handbook**!

In this book, I'll walk you through everything you need to know about worm farming, whether you're looking to improve your garden, reduce waste, or even turn this hobby into a small side business. You don't need a huge backyard or special skills to get started. In fact, all you need are a few worms, some kitchen scraps, and a little bit of patience to see your garden—and maybe even your wallet—thrive.

When I first started, I wasn't exactly sure what to expect. I set up a simple bin, fed the worms some veggie scraps, and went about my day. Fast forward a few weeks, and I had this dark, crumbly compost that made my plants come alive like never before. It didn't take long for me to realize that worm farming isn't just for hardcore gardeners—it's for anyone who wants to turn waste into something valuable, all while helping the planet.

By the time you finish this book, you'll know how to:

- Set up your first worm bin with ease (no fancy equipment required).

- Harvest worm castings (also known as "black gold") to improve your soil and boost plant growth.

- Avoid common mistakes and troubleshoot like a pro.

- Even turn worm farming into a side business, selling castings, worms, or worm bins.

Worm farming isn't just about improving your garden—it's about making a real impact on the environment and adopting a more sustainable way of living. The best part? It's so easy to get started, and once you do, you might just wonder why you didn't start sooner.

Let's dive in. By the end of this book, you'll have all the knowledge and confidence you need to turn kitchen scraps into garden treasure. Let's roll!

Chapter 1: The Basics of Vermiculture

If you've ever gardened before, you know that soil is everything. Healthy soil means strong, vibrant plants. But what if I told you that improving your soil could be as easy as setting up a worm bin and letting nature do the rest?

Worm farming—or **vermiculture**—might sound like something only expert gardeners or environmentalists get into, but trust me, it's surprisingly simple. And the payoff? Huge. You don't need a degree in soil science or a ton of expensive gear to start seeing the benefits. All you need are a few humble worms, some kitchen scraps, and a little bit of patience.

What is Vermiculture?

At its core, vermiculture is the practice of using worms to turn organic waste into **worm castings**, which are often referred to as **"black gold"** by gardeners. These castings are essentially worm poop, but don't let that gross you out—because this "black gold" is packed with nutrients that your garden will love. Worm castings contain beneficial microbes and nutrients that **improve soil structure, enhance plant growth, and help retain moisture.** In other words, worm farming is like having a tiny factory in your backyard that produces the best fertilizer you can get, all while recycling waste that would otherwise end up in the trash.

When I first started, I didn't know much about worms or their role in composting, but it didn't take long to get the hang of it. I set up a simple bin, started feeding them veggie scraps, and in no time, I had rich, dark compost that made my plants look healthier than ever. The best part? It all happened naturally, without much intervention from me. The worms did all the work!

Why Worm Farming Matters

You might be wondering, why worms? Why not just compost like everyone else? Well, here's the thing: worm composting is faster and more efficient than traditional composting. Worms break down organic material quickly, producing nutrient-dense castings in a fraction of the time it would take for a regular compost pile to decompose. Plus, because the process happens in a compact bin, you can do it almost anywhere—whether you have a big backyard, a small patio, or even just a corner in your kitchen.

For anyone who's into **organic gardening** or **sustainable living**, vermiculture is a game-changer. It doesn't just reduce your waste; it turns that waste into something valuable. Instead of throwing out vegetable scraps or coffee grounds, you're feeding your worms and, in return, getting rich compost that improves the health of your soil and the quality of your plants.

The Types of Worms You'll Need

Not all worms are created equal, and not every type of worm will thrive in a composting environment. The most popular type of worm for vermiculture is the **red wiggler** (Eisenia). Red wigglers are composting champions—they thrive in shallow, moist environments and are great at breaking down organic matter quickly.

You might be familiar with earthworms, the ones you see after a rainstorm, but these guys like to burrow deep into the soil. Red wigglers, on the other hand, prefer to stay near the surface where there's plenty of organic matter for them to feed on. That's why they're perfect for a worm bin.

Chapter 2: Setting Up Your Worm Bin

Now that you know the basics of worm farming, it's time to set up your very own worm bin. Don't worry—this is going to be simple. Whether you're using a store-bought bin or making one yourself, the process is pretty straightforward.

Choosing the Right Worm Bin

Before you start tossing veggie scraps to your worms, you'll need to decide on the type of bin you want. There are plenty of options depending on your space and preferences:

- **Plastic Bins**: These are perfect for beginners because they're cheap, easy to find, and simple to set up. You can get a standard plastic storage bin and convert it into a worm bin with just a few modifications.

- **Wooden Bins**: If you prefer a more eco-friendly option, wooden bins are a great choice. They're breathable and help maintain moisture levels better than plastic, but they can break down over time.

- **Stackable Tray Systems**: These are the go-to for serious worm farmers who want something scalable. Tray systems allow worms to move between layers as they compost, making it easier for you to harvest the worm castings from the bottom tray.

Whichever option you choose, the key is to make sure the bin is **well-ventilated** . Worms need air to survive, so you'll need to drill some small holes in the sides of the bin to provide proper airflow.

Preparing the Bedding

Worms don't live directly in the food scraps you give them. Instead, they need **bedding** to nest in and help break down the organic material. Think of the bedding as the foundation of your worm farm—it's where the worms live and work their magic.

For bedding, you can use:

- **Shredded newspaper**: A classic option, newspaper is absorbent and easy to find. Just make sure it's free of glossy pages or colored ink.

- **Coconut coir**: This is a more professional option, made from the husks of coconuts. It's great at holding moisture and breaking down over time.

- **Dried leaves:** If you have a yard full of dried leaves, they make excellent bedding. Just avoid leaves treated with pesticides.

Mix the bedding with a little water until it's moist but not soaking wet, like a damp sponge. Then, spread it evenly in the bin. This will create the perfect environment for your worms to start turning scraps into compost.

Adding Your Worms

Once your bin is ready, it's time to add the stars of the show: the worms. **Red wigglers** are the best choice for most worm bins, and you can easily buy them online or at a gardening store.

Here's what to do:

1. Add about **500–1,000 worms** to your bin. This sounds like a lot, but worms are small and you'll need enough to start the composting process.

2. Scatter the worms over the bedding, and let them settle in. Within a few minutes, they'll start burrowing into the bedding, getting comfortable in their new home.

Feeding Your Worms

Your worms are ready to eat! But what exactly do they like to munch on? Here's a breakdown of what's great for your worms and what to avoid:

- **Good foods**: Fruit and vegetable scraps (apple peels, banana skins), coffee grounds, tea bags, crushed eggshells.

- **Avoid**: Meat, dairy, oils, processed foods, citrus peels (too acidic for worms).

As a general rule, chop or break down large pieces of food before adding them to the bin. Smaller pieces decompose faster, which means the worms can break them down more quickly. Feed your worms about 1-2 pounds of food scraps per week. You'll know they're eating well when the food starts to disappear within a few days.

Troubleshooting Common Issues

Starting your worm bin is easy, but sometimes things can go wrong. Here are a few common problems and how to fix them:

- **Bad smells**: If your worm bin smells bad, it's usually because there's too much food or not enough airflow. Cut back on feeding, and make sure there are plenty of ventilation holes in the bin.

- **Too dry or too wet**: Worms like moisture, but they don't want to swim. If the bin is too wet, add more bedding to absorb the excess moisture. If it's too dry, lightly spray the bedding with water.

- **Worms escaping**: If your worms are trying to leave the bin, it could mean something's wrong with their environment. Check the moisture levels and make sure they're getting enough food.

Chapter 3: Harvesting Worm Castings

One of the most rewarding parts of worm farming is when you get to harvest that beautiful, dark compost—the worm castings—that your worms have been creating. These castings are packed with nutrients, and you can use them to improve the health of your soil and plants. In this chapter, we'll walk through when and how to harvest worm castings, and how to use them effectively in your garden.

When to Harvest Your Castings

So how do you know when your worms have finished processing the food and bedding into rich compost? Here are a few signs to look for:

- **The bedding looks dark and crumbly**: It's no longer the shredded paper or leaves you started with. Instead, it should look more like soil.

- **No large food pieces remain:** Most of the food scraps should be broken down, and the worms should be mostly focused on the remaining bedding.

This process can take anywhere from a few weeks to a couple of months, depending on how many worms you have and how often you feed them. Once the majority of the bin looks like **rich, dark soil**, you'll know it's time to harvest the castings.

How to Harvest Worm Castings

Harvesting worm castings is pretty easy, but it can be done in a few different ways depending on how much you need and how hands-on you want to be. Here are a couple of simple methods:

1. The Manual Method (Ideal for Small Bins)

- If you're working with a small worm bin, the easiest way to harvest is to move the worms and fresh food to one side of the bin.

- On the opposite side, stop adding new food and let the worms finish processing the bedding and scraps.

- After a week or so, most of the worms will migrate to the side with fresh food, leaving the castings behind.

- Scoop out the castings, and voila—you've got your first batch of worm compost!

2. **The Light Method** (Perfect for Outdoor or Open Bins)

- Worms don't like light, so one trick is to empty the contents of the bin onto a tarp or newspaper in bright sunlight.

- The worms will burrow down to escape the light, leaving the top layer of castings free for you to collect.

- After scooping off the top layer, wait a few minutes for the worms to burrow deeper, then collect another layer of castings.

- Repeat until you're left with mostly worms and a bit of unfinished material.

3. **The Tray System** (Best for Larger Operations)

- If you're using a stackable tray system, this process is even easier.

- As worms finish composting one tray, they'll naturally migrate upward to the next tray in search of fresh food.

- You can then remove the bottom tray (which will be filled with castings), add fresh bedding to the top tray, and continue the process.

No matter which method you choose, be sure to leave a little bit of the castings behind in the bin. These castings contain beneficial microbes that will help kick-start the composting process in the next round.

Using Worm Castings in Your Garden

Now that you have your castings, it's time to put them to work in your garden. The great thing about worm castings is that they're rich in nutrients but gentle enough to use on any type of plant. You can use them in several ways:

- **As a soil amendment:** Mix the castings directly into your garden soil to improve its structure and boost its nutrient content. Castings help the soil retain moisture, making it more fertile and less prone to drying out.

- **In potting soil:** Add about 10–20% worm castings to your potting mix for healthier indoor plants. The nutrients in the castings will feed your plants slowly over time, ensuring steady growth.

- **As a top dressing:** If you don't want to mix the castings into the soil, you can also spread a thin layer on top of your garden beds. The castings will gradually work their way into the soil with watering or rain.

- **Make compost tea**: Compost tea is a liquid fertilizer you can make by soaking worm castings in water. Simply add a cup of castings to a bucket of water, let it steep for 24 hours, and you've got a nutrient-rich tea to water your plants with. This is especially great for feeding delicate plants or seedlings.

How Often Should You Harvest?

Most worm farmers can expect to harvest worm castings every 2 to 3 months, but it really depends on how many worms you have and how much food you're giving them. Larger bins with more worms will produce castings faster, while smaller setups may take a bit longer. Keep an eye on the bedding and food levels, and when it looks like rich, crumbly soil, it's time to collect the castings and start the process again.

Chapter 4: Advanced Worm Farming Techniques

Once you've mastered the basics of worm farming, you may start to think about scaling things up. Whether you're expanding your worm farm to produce more castings or managing multiple bins, this chapter will show you how to take your worm farming skills to the next level.

Scaling Your Worm Farm

As you become more familiar with the process, you might notice that your worms are reproducing, your bin is filling up faster, and your plants are thriving. This is a great time to consider expanding your worm farm, especially if you want to produce more castings or even sell them.

Here's how to start scaling:

1. **Add More Worms:** If your bin is processing food quickly, you can gradually increase the worm population by adding more red wigglers. Worms reproduce naturally in your bin, but you can speed up the process by introducing new worms into the mix.

2. **Create Multiple Bins**: When one bin fills up faster than your plants can use the castings, it's time to think about adding a second or even a third bin. This way, you'll always have a fresh supply of castings while allowing the worms in your other bins to keep working.

3. **Use a Tray System:** For more advanced worm farmers, a **stackable tray system** is the easiest way to manage larger amounts of worms and compost. The worms migrate to the top tray as they finish the food in the lower trays, allowing you to harvest castings more efficiently.

Managing Multiple Worm Bins

If you're expanding beyond one bin, managing multiple setups doesn't have to be complicated. In fact, many worm farmers enjoy the flexibility of having different bins for different stages of composting. Here are a few tips:

- **Label your bins**: It's helpful to keep track of which bin is at what stage. Labeling them by the date they were started will make it easier to know when each one is ready to harvest.

- **Stagger feeding schedules**: Feed one bin at a time, and let the others "rest" while the worms finish processing the food. This way, you'll always have a bin ready to harvest.
- **Monitor moisture levels**: The more bins you have, the more you'll need to pay attention to moisture. Make sure each bin has the right amount of moisture to keep your worms happy, and adjust as needed by adding water or dry bedding.

Maintaining the Perfect Environment for Your Worms

As your farm grows, maintaining the right environment for your worms becomes even more important. Here are a few advanced tips for keeping your worms healthy and productive:

- **Temperature Control**: Worms thrive in temperatures between 55°F and 77°F (13°C and 25°C). If you live in a colder climate, consider moving your bins indoors during the winter, or insulating them with straw or blankets. In hot climates, keep your bins out of direct sunlight to avoid overheating.

- **Balance the Carbon to Nitrogen Ratio**: For optimal worm composting, you'll need to maintain the right balance of carbon (bedding materials like shredded paper) and nitrogen (food scraps). Aim for a ratio of about 3 parts carbon to 1 part nitrogen. If the bin smells bad, add more carbon. If it's dry and crumbly, add more nitrogen-rich food scraps.

- **Monitor for Pests**: As your worm farm grows, you may notice pests like fruit flies or mites. Keep them at bay by burying food scraps deeper into the bedding, adding dry bedding to the surface, and covering the bin with a tight-fitting lid. Avoid overfeeding your worms, as this can attract pests.

Composting Different Types of Organic Matter

As you become more advanced in worm farming, you can experiment with different types of organic matter to compost. While food scraps are the most common material, there are plenty of other things your worms can help break down:

- **Shredded cardboard:** Worms love cardboard, and it's a great way to add carbon to the bin.

- **Egg cartons:** Along with shredded paper, egg cartons break down slowly, providing a long-term source of carbon.

- **Hair and fur**: Believe it or not, worms can compost hair and pet fur! Just be sure to add it in small quantities.

- **Dryer lint:** If you use natural fabrics like cotton, dryer lint can be added to your bin as long as it's free from synthetic materials.

By diversifying what you feed your worms, you'll create richer compost and avoid overwhelming the bin with too much of one type of material.

Preparing for Larger-Scale Production

If you're thinking about producing worm castings on a larger scale, there are a few things to consider. Whether you're looking to supply castings for your local community or sell them at farmer's markets, you'll need to ensure that your production process is consistent and your castings are of high quality.

Here's how to get started:

1. **Invest in More Efficient Bins**: Commercial worm farming operations often use larger, industrial bins or flow-through systems that make it easier to manage high volumes of worms and castings.

2. **Market Your Castings**: Start small by selling to friends, neighbors, and local gardening groups. As demand grows, consider expanding to online marketplaces, local garden centers, or farmers' markets. You can even offer castings in bulk to community gardens or organic farms.

3. **Package Your Castings**: If you plan to sell castings, make sure to package them in a way that's appealing to buyers. Small bags of castings are perfect for home gardeners, while larger quantities can be sold to professional growers. Include simple instructions for use to help customers get the most out of the product.

Chapter 5: Turning Worm Farming into a Side Business

For many people, worm farming starts as a simple hobby—a way to improve their garden and reduce waste. But did you know that worm farming can also turn into a **profitable side business**? As demand for organic gardening solutions grows, more people are turning to natural composting methods, and worm castings are at the top of the list.

In this chapter, I'll guide you through the steps to **monetize your worm farm**, whether you want to sell **worm castings, worms,** or even **composting systems**. This side business could provide you with extra income while helping others improve their gardens sustainably.

The Market for Worm Castings

There's a growing awareness among gardeners and farmers that **worm castings** are one of the most effective natural fertilizers available. Rich in nutrients and beneficial microbes, worm castings are used to:

- Boost plant growth.

- Improve soil structure.

- Increase water retention in the soil.

With more people embracing **organic gardening** and **sustainable living**, there's a high demand for worm castings. Home gardeners, community gardens, organic farmers, and even landscape companies are potential customers for your product.

Selling Worm Castings

When you start selling worm castings, you'll want to focus on **quality** and **presentation**. Here's how to get started:

1. **Harvest and Package Castings**: Once your worms have processed enough food scraps, it's time to harvest the castings. To make the product appealing to buyers, package the castings in **sealed bags** that protect them from moisture and contamination. Small bags (1-2 pounds) are perfect for home gardeners, while larger quantities can be sold in bulk to farms or landscapers.

2. **Label Your Product**: Create clear, professional labels that include the benefits of worm castings and simple instructions for use. This is especially important for customers who are new to gardening and may not know how to incorporate castings into their soil.

3. **Set Your Price**: Pricing your castings will depend on your market and the quantity you're selling. Start by researching local and online prices to get a sense of what others are charging. For small bags, you might charge between **$10 and $20** depending on your region, while bulk sales could range from **$50 to $100 or more**.

4. **Sell Locally**: Local sales are a great place to start. Visit **farmers' markets**, local gardening clubs, and community gardens to offer your castings. Word of mouth can quickly spread, and local gardeners will appreciate the availability of high-quality, local worm castings.

5. **Sell Online**: Once you've established yourself locally, consider expanding your reach by selling worm castings online. Platforms like **eBay, Etsy, or even Amazon** allow you to market your product to a larger audience. Just be mindful of shipping costs, especially if selling larger quantities.

Selling Worms

In addition to selling castings, you can also sell **live worms**. Gardeners, composters, and schools often need worms for setting up their own composting systems, and there's always a demand for **healthy red wigglers.**

Here's how to get started:

1. **Build a Stock of Worms**: Over time, your worm population will grow. As your worms reproduce, you can divide the worms and set some aside for sale while keeping enough in your bin to maintain your own composting process.

2. **Package Worms for Shipping**: When selling worms, it's crucial to package them in a way that ensures they arrive alive and healthy. Use breathable containers with a small amount of bedding material and moisture. If selling locally, you can skip the shipping costs by arranging pickup or delivery.

3. **Set Worm Prices**: A pound of red wigglers typically contains 800–1,000 worms and sells for around **$30–$50** depending on demand and your location. You can sell them in smaller quantities as well for people just getting started.

Selling Worm Bins and Composting Systems

If you're handy, another way to expand your business is by **building and selling worm bins***1 or **composting systems**. As more people discover the benefits of vermiculture, they'll need high-quality, easy-to-use setups to get started.

1. **Create Simple Worm Bins**: You can make worm bins out of **plastic containers, wooden crates**, or other eco-friendly materials. Be sure to include proper ventilation and drainage holes, as well as a set of easy-to-follow instructions for setup and maintenance.

2. **Sell Worm Bin Kits**: To make the process even easier for your customers, you can offer **worm bin starter kits** that include the bin, bedding, and a starter batch of worms. This all-in-one package is especially appealing to people who want a hassle-free start to worm farming.

3. **Advertise on Local Platforms**: You can sell these systems through local classifieds like **Facebook Marketplace** or **Craigslist**. Many people prefer to buy from local vendors rather than ordering online and dealing with shipping costs.

Expanding Your Reach: Marketing Tips

Once you've started selling your worm-related products, it's time to think about expanding your reach and growing your customer base. Here are a few simple, cost-effective marketing strategies:

1. **Create a Website**: A basic website can help you showcase your products, explain the benefits of worm farming, and make it easy for customers to contact or purchase from you. It doesn't need to be complicated—a simple site with pictures, product descriptions, and a contact form will do the trick.

2. **Use Social Media:** Platforms like **Instagram, Facebook**, and **Pinterest** are perfect for connecting with gardening enthusiasts and promoting your business. Share photos of your worm farm, before-and-after shots of gardens that have benefitted from your castings, and tips on composting. These visual platforms are great for inspiring others to start their own worm farm while bringing attention to your products.

3. **Partner with Local Garden Centers**: Reach out to local nurseries and garden centers to see if they'd be interested in carrying your worm castings or worm bins. This can open the door to more customers and increase your sales potential without the need for heavy online marketing.

4. **Offer Workshops***l: Consider offering workshops or classes on worm farming at community centers, schools, or gardening clubs. People who attend will be eager to learn, and many will want to purchase worms or worm bins afterward.

Chapter 6: The Role of Worm Farming in Sustainable Gardening

Worm farming is more than just a way to improve your garden—it's part of a larger movement toward **sustainable living**. By turning food scraps into valuable compost and improving the health of your soil, worm farming helps you reduce waste, conserve resources, and create a healthier environment for plants, people, and wildlife.

In this chapter, we'll explore how worm farming fits into the bigger picture of sustainability and how it can be integrated into other eco-friendly gardening practices. Whether you're growing vegetables, flowers, or maintaining a home garden, worm farming can play a central role in creating a garden that thrives without relying on synthetic fertilizers or harmful chemicals.

Why Sustainable Gardening Matters

Sustainable gardening is all about working with nature, not against it. In traditional gardening, many people rely on chemical fertilizers, pesticides, and herbicides to keep their plants healthy and productive. While these products may provide short-term results, they often come with long-term consequences, such as:

Depleting the soil of essential nutrients.

Polluting waterways with runoff.

Killing beneficial insects and disrupting natural ecosystems.

Worm farming offers a solution by providing a natural, eco-friendly alternative to chemical fertilizers. Worm castings are rich in nutrients and microbes that **enhance soil health**, promote **strong plant growth**, and help plants resist disease—all without harming the environment.

By incorporating worm farming into your garden, you're not only feeding your plants; you're also improving the structure of your soil, making it more resilient to drought, and supporting the health of the entire ecosystem in your backyard.

Integrating Worm Farming into a Permaculture System

If you're familiar with **permaculture**, you already know that it's based on designing landscapes that mimic the natural world. Worm farming fits perfectly into permaculture because it's a low-maintenance, sustainable way to recycle organic waste and improve soil fertility.

Here's how to integrate worm farming into your permaculture system:

1. **Use Worm Castings in No-Till Gardens**: No-till gardening preserves the natural structure of the soil by avoiding heavy digging or turning. Worm castings can be added directly to the surface of the soil, where they'll gradually work their way down, feeding your plants and supporting microbial life.

2. **Support Pollinator Plants**: Worm castings improve plant health, and healthy plants are more likely to attract beneficial insects like bees and butterflies. By using worm castings on flowering plants, you'll help create a garden that supports pollinators, which are essential to a thriving ecosystem.

3. **Create Closed-Loop Systems**: In a closed-loop system, nothing goes to waste. Kitchen scraps become food for worms, and the castings produced by the worms go back into the garden to grow food, which creates more scraps for the worms. This natural cycle mimics how ecosystems function in the wild, reducing the need for external inputs like commercial fertilizers.

Reducing Your Carbon Footprint with Worm Farming

One of the most impactful ways that worm farming contributes to sustainability is by reducing your **carbon footprint.** The average household generates a significant amount of food waste each week, and most of it ends up in landfills. As this organic material breaks down in the absence of oxygen, it produces methane—a greenhouse gas that's far more potent than carbon dioxide.

By composting your food scraps with worms, you're diverting waste from landfills and preventing the production of methane. You're also reducing the need for chemical fertilizers, which require energy to produce and transport. Worm farming, therefore, helps you **minimize your impact on the environment** while creating a valuable resource for your garden.

Worm Farming and Water Conservation

Healthy soil holds more water, and worm castings are especially good at improving the water retention capacity of your soil. This means that when you use worm castings, your garden becomes more drought-resistant, reducing the need for frequent watering.

In fact, studies have shown that soil treated with worm castings can hold **up to 10 times its weight in water,** which is a huge benefit during dry spells or in areas with water restrictions.

Here's how worm farming helps conserve water in your garden:

- **Improves soil structure:** Worm castings help loosen compacted soil, allowing water to penetrate deeper and reach plant roots.

- **Increases moisture retention**: The organic matter in castings helps the soil hold onto water longer, reducing evaporation and the need for constant watering.

- **Reduces runoff**: Healthy, well-aerated soil absorbs water more efficiently, reducing surface runoff that can carry away nutrients and pollute nearby waterways.

Closing the Loop on Food Waste

Worm farming is part of a broader effort to reduce **food waste** at home. According to global estimates, roughly one-third of all food produced goes to waste, which not only contributes to methane emissions in landfills but also represents a massive waste of resources—everything from the water and energy used to grow the food to the labor and fuel used to transport it.

By composting food scraps with worms, you're closing the loop on food waste. Instead of letting food rot in a landfill, you're turning it into a **valuable resource** that improves your garden, reduces your environmental impact, and makes your home more sustainable.

The Bigger Picture: Worm Farming as Part of a Sustainable Future

Worm farming may seem like a small step, but it's part of a much larger movement toward living more sustainably. Whether you're using worm castings to grow your own food, reduce waste, or improve your soil, you're contributing to a healthier planet. As more people embrace eco-friendly practices like worm farming, we move closer to a future where waste is minimized, resources are conserved, and the health of our environment is prioritized.

By starting your own worm farm, you're not just creating better soil for your garden—you're joining a community of people who believe in working with nature to create a more sustainable world.

Conclusion: Embrace Worm Farming for a Healthier Future

By now, you've learned everything you need to know about worm farming—from setting up your first bin to harvesting the valuable worm castings that can transform your garden. But more than just a practical guide, this book is about embracing a new way of thinking about waste, sustainability, and the power of nature.

Worm farming is one of the simplest, yet most impactful things you can do to improve your garden, reduce waste, and contribute to a more sustainable lifestyle. Whether you started this journey to grow healthier plants, reduce your household waste, or even explore the potential of a worm farming business, you're on the right path.

Stay Committed to the Process

Like anything in life, worm farming takes time and patience. It's not an overnight miracle, but a natural process that rewards consistency and care. You don't need to have a green thumb to succeed—all you need is a willingness to learn and the knowledge that your efforts are making a difference.

The castings your worms produce are more than just fertilizer; they're a **symbol of the positive impact** you're making your garden and the environment. Each handful of rich, dark compost is a testament to the cycle of life—turning waste into something valuable, just as nature intended.

Your Role in the Sustainability Movement

In choosing to start your own worm farm, you've joined a growing community of people who believe in **sustainable living**. Every time you feed your worms, you're contributing to a system that reduces waste, conserves resources, and supports the health of the planet. Your small action is part of a much larger movement—one that's shaping the future of how we live and grow food.

By continuing to compost with worms, you're helping to create healthier soil, grow stronger plants, and reduce your reliance on chemical fertilizers. These are the kinds of changes that don't just benefit your own garden but the entire ecosystem. As your worm farm grows, so does your impact.

Share Your Success

As you continue your worm farming journey, don't be afraid to share your success with others. Whether it's showing off your lush garden, offering tips to friends and family, or even selling your worm castings to local gardeners, you're spreading the word about an eco-friendly, practical solution that anyone can adopt.

Worm farming is more than a hobby—it's a way to give back to the earth, improve your community, and contribute to a sustainable future. Keep experimenting, keep growing, and keep sharing the benefits of this amazing process.

Thank you for joining me on this journey. Your commitment to worm farming isn't just transforming your garden—it's helping to build a healthier, more sustainable world.

Made in the USA
Monee, IL
10 March 2025

13752033R00017